Cello Time Joggers

Cello accompaniment book

Kathy and David Blackwell

> **Teacher's note**
> These duet parts are written to accompany the tunes in *Cello Time Joggers*. They are an alternative to the piano accompaniments or audio tracks, and are not designed to be used with those items.
>
> We are grateful to Alison Ingram and Claire Saddler for all their help in road-testing these duets.
>
> Kathy and David Blackwell

OXFORD
UNIVERSITY PRESS

OXFORD
UNIVERSITY PRESS

Great Clarendon Street, Oxford OX2 6DP,
United Kingdom

Oxford University Press is a department of the University of Oxford.
It furthers the University's objective of excellence in research, scholarship,
and education by publishing worldwide. Oxford is a registered trade mark of
Oxford University Press in the UK and in certain other countries

ISBN 978-0-19-356331-5

Cover illustration by Martin Remphry

Music and text origination by Katie Johnston
Printed in Great Britain on acid-free paper by
Halstan & Co. Ltd, Amersham, Bucks.

Contents

1. Bow down, O Belinda

American folk tune

2. Under arrest!

KB & DB

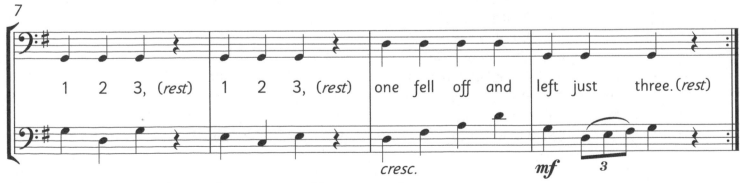

Say the word '*rest*' quietly to yourself as you play.

3. Someone plucks, someone bows

Traditional
Words KB & DB

Down, up goes the bow, when we're play - ing fast or slow;

down, up goes the bow, when we're play - ing high or low.

4. Down up

KB & DB

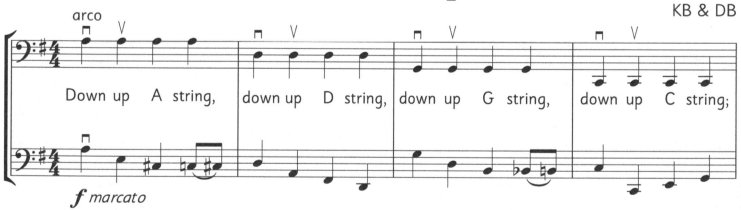

Down up A string, down up D string, down up G string, down up C string;

Play the D and end with G.

* Fill in the letter names of these notes.

5

5. Hill an' gully rider

Trad. Jamaican

6. Fast lane

KB & DB

Try even faster the second time through!

7. In flight

KB & DB

In the rests, let your bow make a circle as you swoop and soar like a bird.

8. Lift off!

KB & DB

Lift your bow off in each of the rests and let it orbit! (Make a circle with your right arm.)

9. Katie's waltz

KB & DB

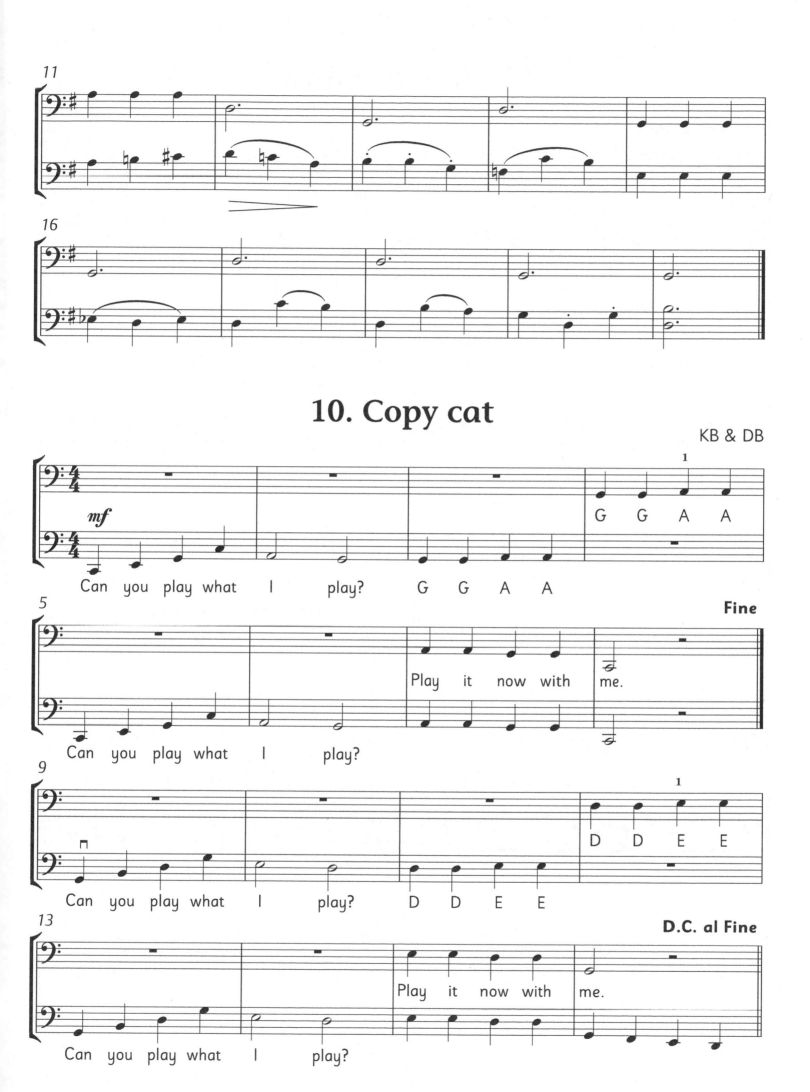

10. Copy cat

KB & DB

11. Rhythm fever

KB & DB

12. Here it comes!

KB & DB

Through the teeth and past the gums, so watch out, tum - my,

here it comes!

Through the teeth and

past the gums, so watch out, tum - my, here it comes!

* Think of a foody rhythm and play it on these notes.

13. Tap dancer

KB & DB

Steadily

D.C. al Fine

* Tap the cello with your left-hand fingers.

14. So there!

KB & DB

So there!

15. Rowing boat

KB & DB

16. Ally bally

Scottish folk tune

17. C string boogie

With a gentle swing

KB & DB

Spin your cello around! *

* Be careful!

18. Travellin' slow

KB & DB

19. Tiptoe, boo!

KB & DB

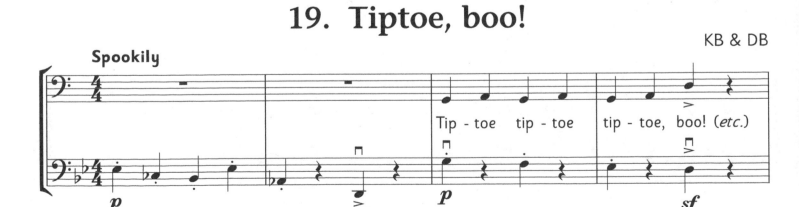

The pupil's part may also be played pizzicato.

20. Lazy cowboy

21. Off to Paris

French folk tune

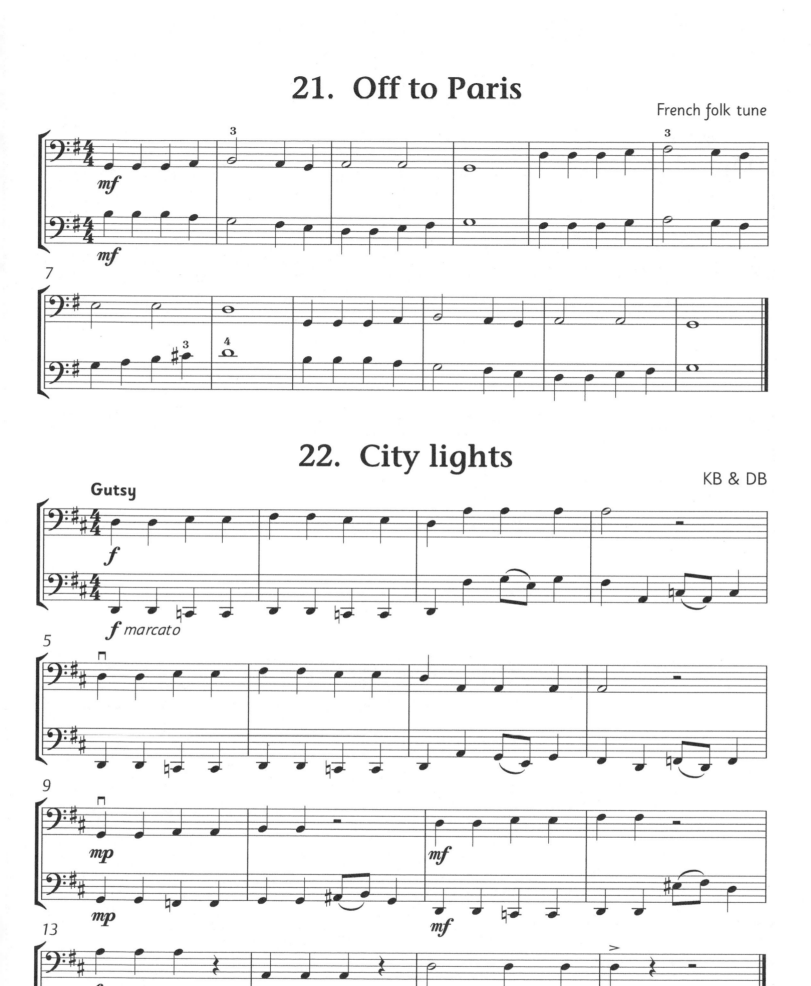

22. City lights

KB & DB

23. Clare's song

KB & DB

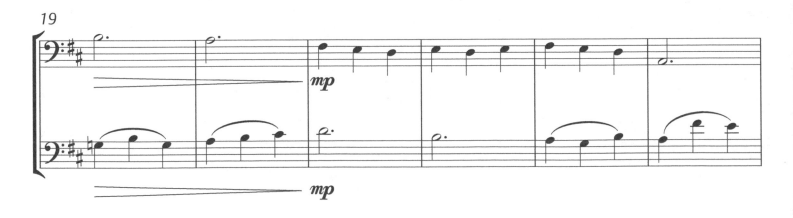

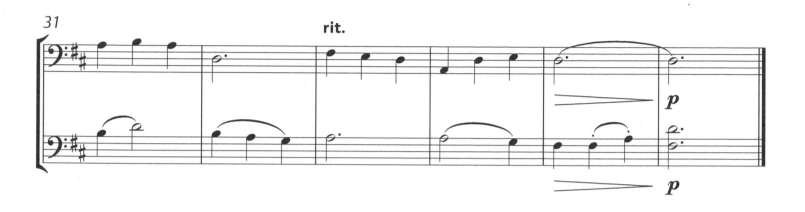

24. Phoebe in her petticoat

American folk tune

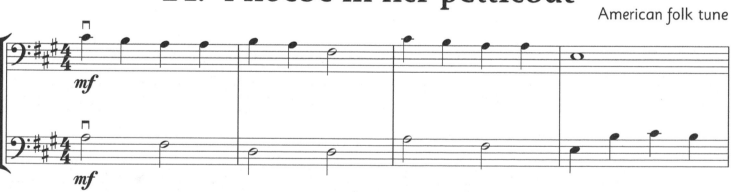

Swap parts when you do the repeat.

25. Peace garden

KB & DB

26. Summer sun

KB & DB

27. On the prowl

KB & DB

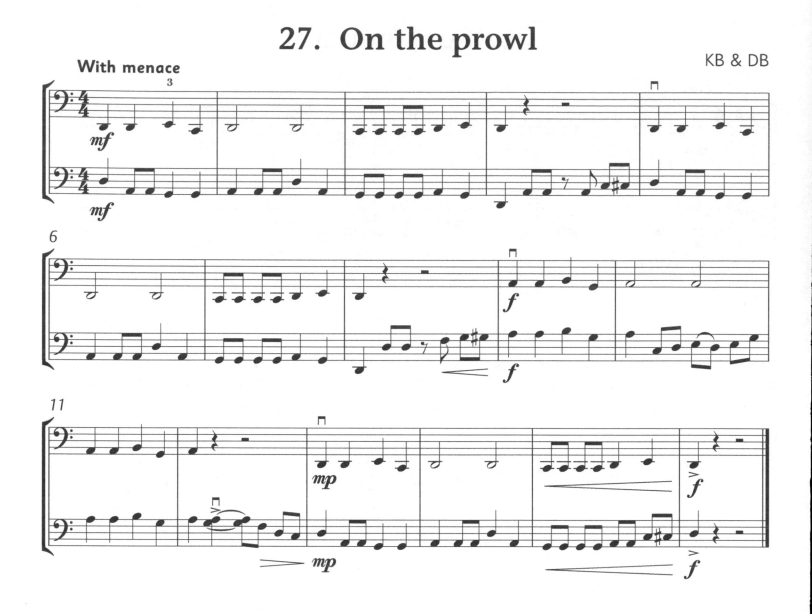

28. Knock, knock!

KB & DB

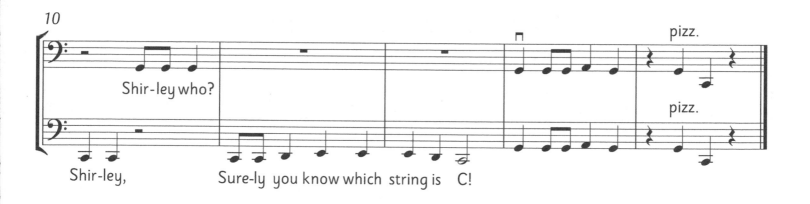

Shir-ley who?

Shir-ley,

Sure-ly you know which string is C!

29. Ready, steady, go now!

KB & DB

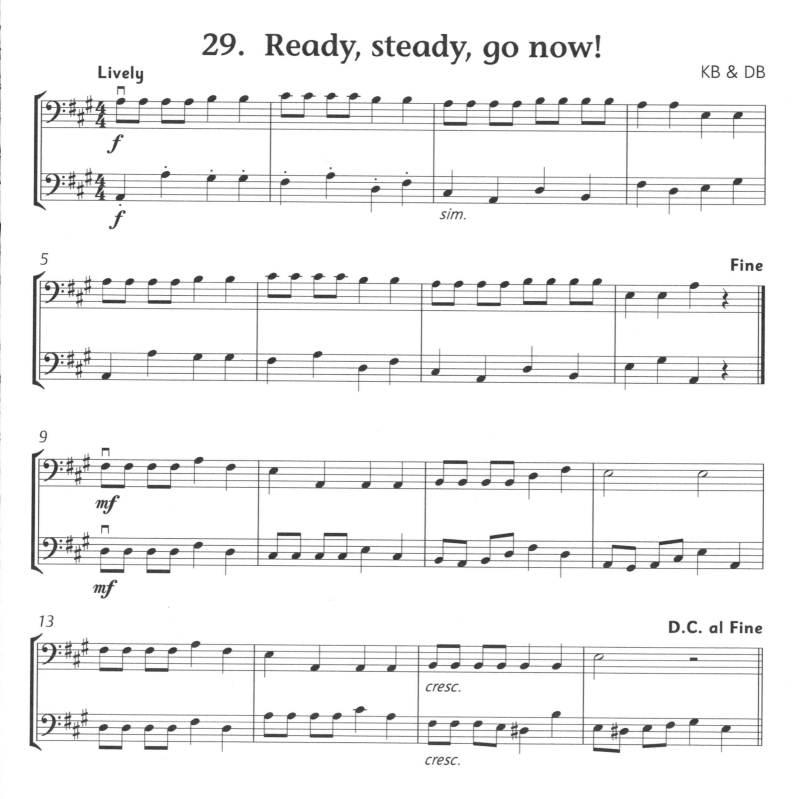

30. Happy go lucky (for Iain)

KB & DB

31. Algy met a bear

KB & DB
Words anon.

Al - gy met a bear, a bear met Al - gy. The

bear was bul - gy, the bulge was Al - gy!

Swap parts when you do the repeat.

32. Listen to the rhythm

KB & DB

33. Cattle ranch blues

KB & DB

34. In the groove

35. Stamping dance

Czech folk tune

36. Walking bass

Slow swing

KB & DB

37. Chopsticks for two

KB & DB

Chunky

38. Runaway train

KB & DB

Express train tempo

39. Distant bells

KB & DB

40. Lazy scale

KB & DB

41. The old castle

With a singing tone

KB & DB

42. Rocking horse

KB & DB

43. Patrick's reel

KB & DB

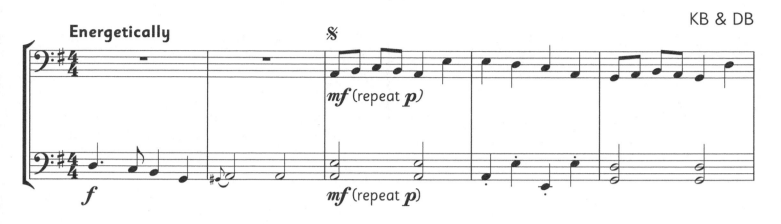

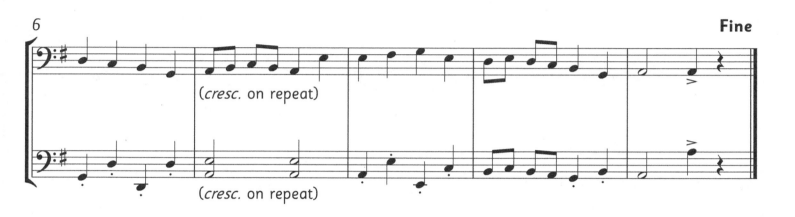

39

44. Calypso time

KB & DB

45. Cello Time

Scaley Things

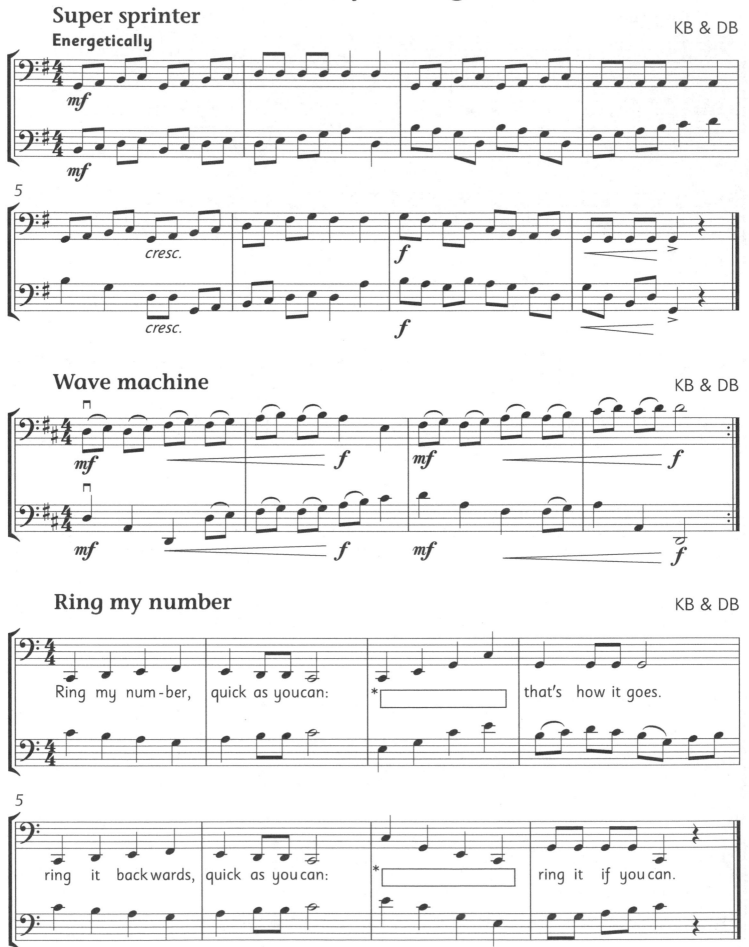

Super sprinter

Energetically

mf

cresc.

f

Wave machine

mf ... *f* ... *mf* ... *f*

Ring my number

Ring my num-ber, quick as you can: * that's how it goes.

ring it back wards, quick as you can: * ring it if you can.

* Use the empty boxes to write in the fingers needed to play these notes.